Omer/Teshuvah

49 Poetic Meditations for Counting the Omer or Turning Toward a New Year

by Shifrah Tobacman

edited by Rachel Barenblat

Second Edition

OMEREMO
NANOPRESS

ISBN 978-0615865829

Omer/Teshuvah (Second Edition)
by Shifrah Tobacman

Editor: Rachel Barenblat

Artwork - "Paper and Light": Elizheva Hurvich

Published by Omeremo Nanopress

Praise for *Omer/Teshuvah*

This book invites us to breathe the air and taste the nectar of the holy, moving through multi-dimensional time, encountering the sacred in the daily. It can be read from one end or the other, offering for our delight, in the words of Gate 38, "a rainbow of colours, a delicious sip of possibilities"!

—*Professor Dr. Ibrahim Farajajé*
Provost and Professor
of Cultural Studies and Islamic studies,
Starr King/Graduate Theological Union.

The poetic images in *Omer/Teshuvah* are lovely and 'meditation provoking'. Through this series of short but powerful thought poems, Shifrah has opened a series of windows to our collective souls, as each of us walks the path of opening gates toward the Holy One of Blessing.

—*Rabbi Min Kantrowitz, author of "Counting the Omer: A Kabbalistic Meditation Guide."*

Shifrah's poems for the days of the *Omer* give new inspirational meaning to the passage between the liberation theme of Passover and the revelation theme of Shavuot. Raising up the motifs of each day and adding to our spiritual practice, this collection guides the reader from a mind-set of scarcity and tentative self-realization through the sea of distraction and self-doubt to a mountain of possibility and spiritual vibrancy. Read these and help make each day count!

—Rabbi Shawn Zevit, teacher, writer, musical artist, spiritual leader and social justice organizer.

Author's Introduction: About the Omer and Omer/Teshuvah

The poetic meditations in this collection are musings from my own practice of counting the *Omer*. The *Omer* is a forty-nine day period between the holiday of *Pesach*, which celebrates freedom, and *Shavuot*, which observes the receiving of Torah. During this time Jews traditionally count each day and recite a special blessing for doing this practice.

I was first introduced to the practice of counting the *Omer* in the 1980's when a visiting rabbi, Yonassan Gershom, led a weekend of teachings for *Lomdim*, a community in Chicago of which I was a member at the time. I was immediately taken by the idea. The practice has a rich cultural history and spiritual resonance that easily blend Judaism's ancient agricultural roots, medeival mystical innovation, and modern social and spiritual sensibilities. It proved to be a perfect combination for me as a spiritual seeker who was, and is, also dedicated to social change.

In 2006, I attended a seminar taught by Rabbi Zalman Schachter-Shalomi. He mentioned the idea of counting in a similar way for the seven weeks that lead up to *Rosh Ha-shana*, the Jewish new year. He had heard of this idea from Cantor Michael Esformes, who recommended counting down from forty-nine at this time. As I began to do this, I found myself writing poems, which turned into meditations, and finally became the substance of this book.

I am using the term *Omer/Teshuvah* or *Omer Teshuvah* for the practice of counting down to the new year. This counting begins immediately following *Tisha B'av*, which commemorates the destruction of the ancient Temple in Jerusalem. The Hebrew word *teshuvah* refers to turning or returning. It is used to describe the process of soul-searching and forgiveness that Jews engage in, particularly during the High Holy Days in the Fall, and during the weeks which precede them.

You are invited to use all or any of the poems here to help you in your own spiritual journey during the *Omer*, or *Omer/Teshuvah*, or at any other time you may find them helpful.

Agricultural Roots, Modern Sensibilities

In Jewish tradition, the counting of the *Omer* represents a period in ancient days when the people would travel to Jerusalem to make offerings from their spring harvest. Seven weeks after the first day of *Pesach* (Passover) they would bring a grain offering to the Temple. Later on, after the destruction of the Temple, people came to observe the end of the seven weeks as the ritual anniversary of receiving the Torah at Mt. Sinai. This observance is the holiday we call *Shavuot*.

These agricultural and communal origins of the *Omer* make it an excellent opportunity for considering our relationship to each other, to the Earth that sustains us, and to the Source of All Life that blesses our own lives each day.

Jewish Mysticism

Jewish mystics of the sixteenth century devised a way to count the *Omer* by invoking seven attributes of God. Each of these attributes, or *sefirot*, is thought to be essential to having a healthy balanced life.

The seven *sefirot* represented in the counting of the *Omer* are:

Loving-kindness (*Chesed*)
Strength, Discipline (*Gevurah*)
Harmony, Beauty (*Tiferet*)
Endurance (*Netzach*)
Splendor, Humility (*Hod*)
Connection, Binding, Foundation (*Yesod*)
Sovereignty, Divine Presence (*Malkhut, Shekhina*)

Each week of the *Omer* is represented by one of these qualities. Each day of the week is as well. So on each day of the *Omer*, a practitioner can focus on two particular qualities.

For example, the third day of each week is symbolized by *Tiferet*, which represents balance, beauty and harmony. The first week is symbolized by *Chesed*, which can be translated as loving-kindness. So on the third day of the first week a practitioner might meditate on what it means to have balance and harmony in their lives, and to have that nestled within loving-kindness.

Each attribute is referred to in kabbalistic literature as a gateway to Divine Presence. These gates are guideposts, an opportunity to re-orient oneself on the trail of life.

How to Count the Omer

Traditionally, the *Omer* is counted in the evening, since sundown is the beginning of the day on the Jewish calendar. The practitioner says a blessing, and then announces the day that is being counted.

The traditional blessing is:

בָּרוּךְ אַתָּה יְיָ, אֱלֹהֵינוּ מֶלֶךְ הָעוֹלָם, אֲשֶׁר קִדְּשָׁנוּ בְּמִצְוֹתָיו וְצִוָּנוּ אַל סְפִירַת הַעֹמֶר.

> *Baruch ata YHVH, eloheynu melech ha-olam, asher kidshanu b'mitzvotav vitzivanu al sefirat ha-omer.*

> Blessed are You, YHVH, our God, Sovereign of the Universe, that sanctifies us with the holy deed of counting the *Omer*.

8

There are many calendars available that can help you keep track of the day. I highly recommend the book *Counting the Omer: A Kabbalistic Meditation Guide* by Min Kantrowitz. It is a highly practical and informative resource filled with rich spiritual teachings and guidance for counting the *Omer*.

Using These Meditations

Some people find that it serves them best to use the meditations in the evening. Others use them in the morning as a way to set an intention for their activities that day. Still others dip into the poems as needed for support on their spiritual journey. Experiment, and find what works for you. That is how you will make meaning from this process and reap the benefits of the *Omer*'s rich spiritual soil.

A Note On Omer/Teshuvah

To count *Omer* Teshuvah, go straight to the end of the book and make your way back to the beginning.

The Love of the Journey

You will find that there are two poems representing *Chesed* within *Chesed* (loving-kindness within itself.) This quality is the focus at the beginning of the *Omer* journey, and the end of *Omer Teshuvah* count. One of these poems is meant for counting the *Omer*; the other, for counting *Omer Teshuvah*. It is my hope that these and other meditations in this collection can serve as guideposts and reminders of the love and discovery which are always available to us when we pay attention.

May your spirit be nurtured by kindness and curiosity, and your life be filled with the blessings of freedom, wisdom, and an ever-deepening connection to the world around you, now and always.

Art By Elizheva Hurvich

The evocative folded paper and light studies by Elizheva Hurvich are noteworthy. When asked if she would provide drawings for this book, the artist first made a number of sketches in an attempt to capture the sense of spiritual journey one experiences in counting the Omer. Gates and pathways were her motifs. When her sketches didn't produce the results she was looking for, Elizheva began folding paper and photographing it for inspiration. Playing with the light and shadow she noticed something special. The result is the artwork found in this book, which adds yet another interesting and surprising dimension to this multi-faceted spiritual adventure.

From the Editor

Shifrah Tobacman and I met as students in DLTI (the Davvenen Leadership Training Institute), a two-year training program in liturgical leadership offered at Elat Chayyim, the Jewish Renewal retreat center, at that time located in Accord NY and now part of the program of Camp Isabella Freedman in CT. Sometime after DLTI, I encountered her Omer poems for the first time.

Shifrah's Omer poems moved me the very first time I read them: not so much as poetry qua poetry, but as devotional exercises, as the expression of a soul yearning for greater connection with the divine.

Counting the Omer—the 49 days between Pesach and Shavuot, between liberation and covenant—is a spiritual practice I've come to cherish. I love the way it sanctifies the passage of time. The kabbalistic interpretations of each week and each day in the journey offer lenses through which my springtime journey is reflected and refracted each year. From the day of *chesed* (lovingkindness) squared through the day of *Shekhinah* (immanent divine presence / Kingdom) squared, each day takes on its own spiritual tone.

When I learned that the count can be done in the reverse order during the seven weeks between Tisha b'Av (our day of communal mourning) and Rosh Hashanah (the Jewish

New Year) at the far pole of the Jewish festival year, I found the practice even more fascinating and revelatory. These seven weeks, taken together, offer a picture of what some Hasidim call "descent for the sake of ascent" — from the spiritual depths of 9 Av, we are newly able to make the spiritual ascent into and through the month of Elul to the Days of Awe. And when we count the days between them, we link our day of communal sorrow with a process of individual *teshuvah* (repentance / return.)
I love that Shifrah's manuscript is intended to be used at both seasons, to help readers mindfully sanctify both of these journeys through Jewish sacred time.

We had fun conceptualizing how the layout of this book might work so that it could be read front-to-back (Omer) or back-to-front (Omer Teshuvah.) Held one way, this is bound like an English-language book; held the other way, it's bound like a Hebrew-language book. In this, the book manifests the dual identity with which so many Diaspora Jews are familiar.

And, of course, there's always the famous saying about Torah "Turn it and turn it, for everything is in it." (Pirkei Avot 5:26) This book, too, is meant to be turned and re/turned.

This book is rooted simultaneously in two worlds, the world of poetry and the world of prayer. Poetry and liturgy are, of course, close cousins; much of the classical Jewish liturgy takes poetic form. But the needs of a poem and the needs of a prayer aren't always identical.

The work in this manuscript is, I think, primarily aligned with the needs of prayer. Following in the footsteps of our mutual teacher Reb Zalman Schachter-Shalomi, Shifrah has written poems which are meant to be prayed.

In the poem for Gate 39, Shifrah writes, "What do you use / to keep yourself connected / to God?" With these lines, and with so many others in this collection, she reminds me to enter spiritual practice wholly. "We use the tools at our disposal / to put the pieces back together," begins the poem for Gate 41. May this collection help each of us to put our pieces back together, and to reassemble the shards of a creation which is always ready for repair.

Rabbi Rachel Barenblat

Folded paper and light study, "Shaft of Wheat," Elizheva Hurvich, 2012.

Poems for Counting the Omer

If you wish to count
from *Tisha b'Av* to *Rosh Hashanah*
please turn to the other end of the book.

Gate 1
Chesed b'Chesed / Loving-kindness
within Loving-kindness

BEGINNING:
COUNTING THE OMER
WEEK 1, DAY 1

Take a breath. Look around.
Hear the shofar beckon
from another time of year.
Awaken to it. Let it open you to beauty,
even in difficult times.

Take in the goodness
that surrounds you.
Kindness rests within kindness.
This is the platform
from which we begin
the ascent to Shavuot.

Notice the journey
you have already taken.
Look back at the terrain.
Remember its variations,
its constancies.

Turn again and look ahead.
The mountain on the horizon
is your heart's deepest wisdom.
Take time to notice
its shape and size from afar,
the path to reach it.

Feel the ground beneath your feet,
trust the earth which holds you,
the Universal Generosity
which contains within it all the kindnesses
you have ever known,
or could want to know.

Step up to the first gate,
cross the threshold
and see what awaits.

Please note:

The poem for Gate One is found here in two versions.

For counting the Omer period, start with the poem on page 18.

If you are counting Omer/Teshuvah, the last poem before Rosh Ha-Shanah is on page 20.

Gate 1
Chesed b'Chesed / Loving-kindness within Loving-kindness

AT THE CUSP OF ROSH HA-SHANAH
OMER TESHUVAH
WEEK 7, DAY 7

Take a breath. Look around.
Elul is almost over.

Hear the shofar.
Awaken to it. Let it open you to beauty
even in difficult times.

Take in the goodness
that surrounds you.
Kindness rests within kindness.
This is the platform
from which we begin a new year.

But first, coast on this gentle slope.
Take time for yourself to do this.

Look back at the journey
you have taken.
Consider inviting a friend to join you.
Drink in the vista together.

Feast on the ripe harvest
of your hearts' planting.
You are ready to get ready.

Turn to face the New Year,
here at the very first gate.

Please note:

The poem for Gate One is found here in two versions.

For counting the Omer period, start with the poem on page 18.

If you are counting Omer/Teshuvah, the last poem before Rosh Ha-Shanah is on page 20.

Gate 2
Gevurah b'Chesed / Discipline
within Loving-kindness

OMER
WEEK 1, DAY 2

OMER TESHUVAH
WEEK 7, DAY 6

Some learnings come to us like puzzles
that are difficult to piece together.
Some come like an idyllic painting
that we can understand immediately.

Some relationships are tricky to maneuver
filled with jagged edges that cut us
while some are so soft and rounded we can
barely tell
where one person ends and the other begins.

Gevurah is strength which keeps us intact,
helps us maintain our integrity,
without which even our love
can become self-destructive.

What keeps you intact?
What helps you be honest with yourself
and with others?

These are things to cherish
as you cross through the 2nd gate.

Gate 3
Tiferet b'Chesed / Beauty and Harmony within Loving-kindness

OMER
WEEK 1, DAY 3

OMER TESHUVAH
WEEK 7, DAY 6

Sometimes we are blessed with balance.
Sometimes we can create that blessing
by pouring sorrow, regret, pain and loss
into a loving container of transformation
to then be poured back out
into our lives.

When we are hurt or angry
it can be difficult to hold others lovingly,
to see the container that can hold our love.
This may be a private matter, or communal.
Either way, courage,
and emotional alchemy, are required.

The container must be strong enough,
large enough, steady enough
to safely hold volatility.

Notice what you need.
The tone of discussion,
the physical setting, the emotional milieu,
the people supporting you,
the opening of your own heart.

Imagine pouring in all your love,
and a willing partner
pouring theirs in as well.

Let it wash over you,
carry you,
through the 3rd gate.

Gate 4
Netzach b'Chesed / Endurance
within Loving-kindness

OMER
WEEK 1, DAY 4

OMER TESHUVAH
WEEK 7, DAY 4

A Muslim man in Jerusalem
has devoted himself to healing
deep fissures in his region.

Muslims, Jews and Christians,
Buddhist monks, Hindu devotees,
Native American shamans:
he welcomes and brings us all to his house.
His wife gives us tea and shares food with us.
He and his partners for peace
travel the world, climbing the rocky pathways
of reconciliation.

Healing relationships can take time,
endurance.

What relationship would you like
to see healed?
What relationships can you help mend
in the world?
What is the first step you can take
toward *tikkun olam*,
the healing transformation of the world
to one that is more loving and just?

It may be a tiny shift
in your most intimate circle

or a simple gesture of caring
for the broader world around you.

In your heart, make yourself a promise.

In your mind's eye
take a stand and take a step
through the 4th gate.

Gate 5
Hod b'Chesed / Humility and Splendor
within Loving-kindness

OMER
WEEK 1, DAY 5

OMER TESHUVAH
WEEK 7, DAY 3

A small polished geode
with blue striations like deep water
rests in your hand. It is soothing,
like the pools of a lover's eyes.

There is an opening on its front
a simple gray depression,
but look more closely:
see how it sparkles inside,
an entire dazzling universe
awaiting your unfolding presence,
Your Unfolding Presence.

You notice the oneness
of the gray iridescence,
the edge where the rough inner light
meets the deep color
of the external polished stone.

Imagine kindness surrounds you,
envelopes you. Whose face does it wear?
With what colors does it appear?

What spark in you is teased out
by the presence of this great kindness?

What light in you is so powerful
it can't be extinguished
even when kindness withdraws?

Be honest and loving with yourself
here at the 5th gate.

Gate 6
Yesod b'Chesed / Connection within Loving-kindness

OMER
WEEK 1, DAY 6

OMER TESHUVAH
WEEK 7, DAY 2

"Hello, God. How ya doing?"

We all have a direct line to Love
but we have to call in the number.

The loving thing isn't always easy,
And may require dedication.

When we dedicate ourselves
we bind our hearts not only to each other
but also to the Divine,
and that love comes back to us
again and again.

How will you say hello to the Divine today?
How will you say hello to a loved one
in a way that lets them know
you truly love them?

Say "hello" and let your greeting propel you
through the 6th gate.

Gate 7
Malkhut b'Chesed / Divine
Omnipresence within Loving-kindness

OMER
WEEK 1, DAY 7

OMER TESHUVAH
WEEK 7, DAY 1

We are making our way slowly
from the freedom of leaving the narrow place
to the freedom that comes with wisdom.

The worlds are about to fold
one into the next, not to disappear,
but to nestle within each other,
be made whole by their connection.

The grandiose sovereignty of ego gone astray
can loosen the edges of its power,
fold into the simplicity of a kind word,
a random act of loving-kindness,
a moment of forgiveness.

What control will you relinquish,
what idea will you unfasten,
what assumption will you decree annulled
to make space in your heart
for goodwill to enter freely
and pour out willingly?

Make this space in you now
here at the 7th gate.

Folded paper and light study, Elizheva Hurvich, 2012.

Gate 8
Chesed b'Gevurah / Loving-kindness within Discipline

OMER
WEEK 2, DAY 1

OMER TESHUVAH
WEEK 6, DAY 7

Be kind to the structure
that houses you.

Install a double paned window
for better insulation and UV protection.
You may have to repaint the trim.
Enjoy the light pouring through.

Warm your home
with family and friends,
whatever the season.

Kindness to your self
can be kindness to Her,
to All.

Cross through the 8th gate
just outside your door.

Gate 9
Gevurah b'Gevurah / Discipline within Discipline

OMER   **OMER TESHUVAH**
WEEK 2, DAY 2   **WEEK 6, DAY 6**

The sod is laid neatly in a rounded pattern
in a small area of the carefully designed yard.

Stepping stones encircle it,
small grasses, flowering plants, woolly thyme.
An intimate portrait is drawn,
three concentric circles embrace one another,
warmth, love, determination.

At night the raccoons come
for a midnight snack
of the grubs beneath the sod.
Their adept determined claws
lift the sod neatly at the corners
folding it back like little blankets
to expose what's beneath.
In the morning the people grumble
as they re-place the sod,
tuck it back within its tidy borders.
Next night the raccoons return.

The people try everything they can think of
to secure their borders;
cayenne pepper, water spray,
netting secured with tent stakes.
Nothing works until they stake the net so tight
that mowing takes an hour.

One day the raccoons grow tired of this game,
go elsewhere. The grass takes hold.

What do you need to grow safely?
What do you need to eat
and what can you forego
to allow the growth of others?

Move thoughtfully, taking care
not to trip on the netting,
and make your way through the 9th gate.

Gate 10
Tiferet b'Gevurah / Balance
and Harmony within Discipline

OMER
WEEK 2, DAY 3

OMER TESHUVAH
WEEK 6, DAY 5

The young martial artist stands perfectly still,
one leg bent high in front of him,
arms up like wings
in the pose of a crane, perched upon a post
with the ocean before him
the sound of waves that could be distracting
without discipline, but which instead
pose infinite possibilities.

How did he get to this place?

Practice, devotion, the love
of a thoughtful mentor.

Imagine climbing a stairway.
At the top there's a door.
You knock and are greeted
by someone wise: your own Inner Sage,
a perfectly balanced version
of your most fulfilled self.

Take in the being before you,
and the surroundings
in which you find yourself.

Ask a question.
Wait for an answer.
Say thank you.

Walk back down the stairs
and through the 10th gate
committed to your own inner beauty.

Gate 11
Netzach b'Gevurah / Endurance
within Discipline

OMER	OMER TESHUVAH
WEEK 2, DAY 4	**WEEK 6, DAY 4**

Things that last
within things that hold

our communications few and far between
and yet
when I arrive on your doorstep,
dinner is ready, a place set for me,
and our hearts warm,
as if we had never finished the last
conversation

netzach sh'b'gevurah,
the 11th gate.

*This poem was contributed to the collection
by Elizheva Hurvich.*

Gate 12
Hod b'Gevurah / Humility and Splendor
within Discipline

OMER
WEEK 2, DAY 5

OMER TESHUVAH
WEEK 6, DAY 3

Transformation can be breathtaking
and yet its unfoldings go unnoticed.

A caterpillar winds its cocoon,
blending with its environment
while the mysterious process of re-creation
unfurls itself within.

It waits for months,
and when its old parts are no longer needed
and its wings are fully formed
it patiently pokes its way back
through the very container
it created for protection, and flies away.

But that isn't the end of its journey.
It might use its new mode of transport
to carry its small body thousands of miles
on the skyway of its forebears
a path imprinted in its being
like the bold colors of it wings.

Transformation, in the end, is breathtaking.

Once it has occurred,
the change may be used to connect to those
who have come before us,
those around us now,
and those who will follow.

Consider a change you are making
or wish to make.
What people or circumstances
or internal discipline do you need?
How can you hold yourself tenderly
as you wait for the "aha"
of flying away on new wings?

Wait a while at the 12th Gate
and behold the splendor
that awaits you.

Gate 13
Yesod b'Gevurah / Connection
within Discipline

OMER   **OMER TESHUVAH**
WEEK 2, DAY 6   **WEEK 6, DAY 2**

Yesod is a connecting force,
creating new life,
exciting, forceful, untested.

Gevurah creates boundaries
for healthy relationship,
lends shape to ideas,
provides safety for otherwise
unbridled energy.

Sparks of new life within you
are borne of an inkling, a thought
a tiny flame in your heart,
a flicker of recognition.

What do you wish to create?
What relationship do you wish to forge,
or deepen, or clarify?

Feel your desire build.
Let your idea take shape.

Notice what is involved
in taking the first step
through this, the 13th gate.

Gate 14
Malkhut b'Gevurah / Divine Presence
within Discipline

OMER
WEEK 2, DAY 7

OMER TESHUVAH
WEEK 6, DAY 1

Today could be a day
to pray with your feet.

What are you doing today?

What blessing would you like
for today's activities?

Whether you are doing something
small or large,
private or public,
alone or with others,
what do you need
to be fully present in this moment
to the life you are living
and the world in which you live?

Offer yourself a blessing
and step through the 14th gate.

Folded paper and light study, Elizheva Hurvich, 2012.

Gate 15
Chesed b'Tiferet / Loving-kindness
within Beauty and Harmony

OMER　　　　　　**OMER TESHUVAH**
WEEK 3, DAY 1　　　**WEEK 5, DAY 7**

Loving-kindness perfectly balanced,
chesed wrapped in *tiferet*.

Notice your own gifts.
Wrap them beautifully
and give them to yourself.

Be gentle with your self.
Commit random acts of loving-kindness
on your behalf.

Hold yourself tenderly
in your own sweet thoughts
under the perfectly balanced archway
of the 15th gate.

Gate 16
Gevurah b'Tiferet / Disciplined strength
within Beauty and Harmony

OMER   **OMER TESHUVAH**
WEEK 3, DAY 2   **WEEK 5, DAY 6**

February, 2004 - thousands of couples
line up at San Francisco City Hall,
join the call to love and justice
put out by the Mayor
to same-sex couples everywhere.
Hosts of lovers, ranks of revelers!

The power is palpable.
A blanket of blessing
warms the entire city.

Gevurah is the discipline needed
to win wars. Could we
transform *gevurah* so thoroughly
that hundreds of people lined up
in a long string of pairs and clusters
would never foretell destruction,
but would instead be assumed a harbinger
of harmonious intimacy,
compassionate discipline,
steadfast communion?

How do you, how can we,
create connections that line up
in the name of both justice and love?

Pose this question to yourself
or ask someone else.
Link arms and march together
through the 16th Gate.

Gate 17
Tiferet b'Tiferet / Balance and Harmony within Balance and Harmony

**OMER
WEEK 3, DAY 3**

**OMER TESHUVAH
WEEK 5, DAY 5**

One night the round moon
kissed the water with light and said,
"You are so beautiful I can barely speak,"
and the water, enchanted
by the moon's reflection,
said, "Kiss me again
and your words will spill out
and I will know exactly what you are thinking."

And the moon kissed the water again
and everything that was in her heart
spilled onto the water,
and the moon and the water
have been dancing ever since.

Sometimes we need to listen deeply to another
to know the love in our own hearts.

Keep your listening heart open today
and be prepared to share what's there
as you travel through the 17th Gate.

Gate 18
Netzach b'Tiferet / Endurance
within Balance and Harmony

OMER
WEEK 3, DAY 4

OMER TESHUVAH
WEEK 5, DAY 4

Y-H-V-H is Be-ing,
It endures.
That is the nature of Being.

You are a spark of the Divine,
"a good thought in the Divine mind",
no more,
no less.

What do you love
about your own enduring nature?

Carry your beautiful self
through this, the 18th Gate.

Gate 19
Hod b'Tiferet / Humility and Splendor
within Balance and Harmony

OMER
WEEK 3, DAY 5

OMER TESHUVAH
WEEK 5, DAY 3

Hod is dazzling in its stillness
like the sun rising brilliant on clear water,
reflecting and bouncing in a v-shaped streak,
mesmerizing yet impossible
to look at for long.

Tiferet is a blue sky laced with white clouds
when the sun is just high enough
to have warmed the earth
but not yet overhead
and there are plenty of shady spots
for those who want them
and places to sit exposed
for those wishing to bake off the morning chill.

Hod sitting within *tiferet*
is like the passion of new love
nestled in the comfort
of a longstanding relationship.
Each can occur and re-occur,
re-ignite, sustain us.

What lights your fire?
What sustains you?

Hold these in your heart
as you travel through the 19th Gate.

Gate 20
Yesod b'Tiferet / Connection
within Balance and Harmony

OMER
WEEK 3, DAY 6

OMER TESHUVAH
WEEK 5, DAY 2

Grasses grow curly and straight.
Sometimes one comes up from its shaft
and wraps itself around a branch, or a lily pad,
or the paddle of a canoe.

Hair grows curly and straight,
its proclivity to wind
determined first by the shaft,
then by humidity and human intervention.

Like grass, hair can be thick or thin,
shiny and smooth, or coarse and crinkly.

Grass grows
because of its attachment to the earth.
Our hair grows
because of its attachment to us.

If grass, where it grows
is like the earth's hair,
our hair, when it grows
is like the body's grassy layer,
protective and decorative,
notable in its presence, or absence.

We may like our hair, or absence thereof,
or not, but there it is,
attached to us, and since we are attached to it
and spring from the Source of Life,
it, and we, grow in harmonious balance.

From what source
 does your own growth appear?
In what ways can you see its beauty?
To what attachments do you attribute
the unique directions of your life?

Wind your way through the grasses
here at the 20th Gate.

Gate 21
Malkhut b'Tiferet / Divine Presence within Balance and Harmony

OMER
WEEK 3, DAY 7

OMER TESHUVAH
WEEK 5, DAY 1

The blue heron is such a graceful pterodactyl,
flapping out of the grasses
she rustles, announces raucously to kayakers
that she is about to take flight,
in a flash she's aloft on powerful wings
her blue feathers indescribable
in the morning or evening light.

She is not perfection, but she is majestic,
balanced, perfectly attuned to her
surroundings.

The Shekhina's wings are bold and broad,
the 21st gate is lofty, stunning.
Imagine Her carrying you
from the thick grasses to the sky in seconds
through the dazzling sunlit opening.

Folded paper and light study, "Shaft of Wheat," Elizheva Hurvich, 2012.

Gate 22
Chesed b'Netzach / Loving-kindness
within Endurance

OMER
WEEK 4, DAY 1

OMER TESHUVAH
WEEK 4, DAY 7

Sometimes we are so frustrated
with the state of the world
or the state of our lives
that anger begets anger.

If violence and war are built
on existing social structures and thoughts,
then peace can be built the same way.

We might start by nurturing
thoughtful hearts
and heartful intelligence.

The energy fields of our physical hearts
extend several feet from our bodies.
Our physical hearts connect
whether our emotional hearts
are ready or not.

If we're not conscious, we crash.
If we approach each other consciously
we can feed the best in one another.

How can you use the energy
of your loving heart
in service to collective well being
and intelligent connection?

Send your heart and brain a message
to expect you at the 22nd gate.

Gate 23
Gevurah b'Netzach / Discipline
within Endurance

OMER
WEEK 4, DAY 2

OMER TESHUVAH
WEEK 4, DAY 6

When you ride a bicycle
in windy conditions
you can minimize the impact
or use the wind to your advantage.

Keep your torso low, eyes straight ahead
when going against the wind
or when the wind is buffeting you from the side
so it flows over you like water off a duck's back.

When the wind is at your back
don't forget to enjoy the ride.
If going downhill
be sure to say "whee!"

If your climb is steep and long
and you have run through
all the gears on your bike
and you are tired
and still need to reach your destination
remember you can always get off and walk.

And if you can't ride a bike,
or use your legs to walk,
you may still find a way
to traverse the windy passage.

Consider the winds on your path today,
the ascents and descents,
and ride, or walk, or otherwise travel
through the 23rd Gate.

Gate 24
Tiferet b'Netzach / Balance and Harmony within Endurance

OMER
WEEK 4, DAY 3

OMER TESHUVAH
WEEK 4, DAY 5

An acrobat, lithe and muscular
winds her body about a rope
tied to a swing, many feet up in the air.

We watch spellbound from the seats below
awed as she balances from the swing
by the back of her slender, well-toned neck.

But you don't have to be an acrobat
to consider the relationship
of balance and coordination,
strength and flexibility.

Most of us are satisfied with simpler feats
of winding our way through the obstacle course
of our days, of bringing our slender
or robust selves, with grace or clumsiness
to the next event, panting,
unsure if we'll make it,
surprised when we do.

Stop to breathe.

What does balance mean to you?
What sort of strength do you need
to endure the life before you
with a sense of equilibrium,
or to be inspired
by your own tenacity?

Sit with this thought
and consider your next step,
then pass through the 24th Gate.

Gate 25
Netzach b'Netzach / Endurance
within Endurance

OMER
WEEK 4, DAY 4

OMER TESHUVAH
WEEK 4, DAY 4

In the middle of our counting
comes this day focused
on endurance within endurance.
What are you enduring today?
What endures on your behalf?

What type of emotional landscape
are you traveling through?
How is it Godly?
What challenges does it pose?

Maybe your journey is one of long flat plains
expanding as far as the eye can see
with each day's trek so much like the last
that when you look back
you aren't certain you've moved at all.

Maybe yours is a narrow trail
winding around the steep mountain
with so many new vistas
it makes your head spin,
the thin air leaving you breathless.

Perhaps yours is a long series
of hills and valleys
with gentle climbs and declines.

Whatever the landscape may be,
what deep joy or learning
can you find along the way?

Look out at the horizon
and drink in what it shows you
then down at the ground beneath you,
shift your weight, sensing the shift,
take a deep breath in and a slow breath out.

Behold the journey ahead of you
here at the 25th Gate.

Gate 26
Hod b'Netzach / Humility and Splendor
within Endurance

OMER
WEEK 4, DAY 5

OMER TESHUVAH
WEEK 4, DAY 3

Hod within *netzach*,
splendor within endurance,
is a gorgeous garment made of tough fabric
that lasts and lasts,
and when it finally gives out,
it biodegrades to renew the earth.

Consider an intricate and colorful
piece of embroidery
stitched on thick linen
with impeccable precision,
one you can tell took great focus and time
for the artisan to realize.
Consider the first thing
the artist might have done
to prepare for this work:
what materials were required,
what kind of studio or space,
what sorts of assistance?

Think of something you are proud of,
something that took time and focus,
even something small,
and when you were done
it was a pleasure to sit back and say
"ah, I am so very pleased
at how this turned out."

What is the very next thing you will do
with a vision of beauty, an intention
to nurture your life and feed your world?

Wear your intention like a garment
to protect and adorn your vision
as you travel through the 26th Gate.

Gate 27
Yesod b'Netzach / Binding
within Endurance

OMER
WEEK 4, DAY 6

OMER TESHUVAH
WEEK 4, DAY 2

When the Great Oneness spoke
the opening Word
from the undivided All of Nothingness,
the world in which we live was created.

We are bound to the Word of creation.

We are bound by our word as well.
When we make a promise to someone
it is considered the *menschlich* thing,
the honorable thing,
to keep that promise.

When we create an intention with our words
a chain of events is set in motion
and when we break the agreement
we risk the bonds of the relationships
on which we depend.

We re-create godliness
each time we keep a holy intention
reminding us again of the link
between our words
and the first Word.

What is one word that represents
your holy intention today?
Write it down, or hold it quietly
in your thoughts
as you pass through the 27th Gate.

Gate 28
Malkhut b'Netzach / Divine Presence
within Endurance

**OMER
WEEK 4, DAY 7**

**OMER TESHUVAH
WEEK 4, DAY 1**

We are turning and returning
at any given moment, *teshuvah.*

Each time we look in a loved one's eyes,
each time we say "I'm sorry" truthfully,
each time we forgive another honestly,
each time we are kind and forgiving
with ourselves,
each time we lay our head down at night
and say,
"I am so grateful for all you
and You have given me today",
with each encounter we are returning.

Walking with meaning takes endurance
and the helping hands of others.

Whose hand would you like to hold?
Who would you like present with you
in body or spirit
as you make your way mindfully
through the 28th gate?

*Folded paper and light study, Elizheva
Hurvich, 2012.*

Gate 29
Chesed b'Hod / Loving-kindness
within Humility and Splendor

OMER   **OMER TESHUVAH**
WEEK 5, DAY 1   **WEEK 3, DAY 7**

Each Hebrew letter has a life of its own.

In the letters that form the word *Hod*
the first letter is *"Hey"* (ה),
pronounced like an English "H".

H-H-H-H-H...

The *hey* breathes out through the broad and
surprising "Oh!"
created by the vowel sound in the middle.

"HO!"

Then the breath comes out
through the end letter, *Dalet* (ד),

Dalet, meaning "doorway",
pronounced like an English "D".

HOD!

Then the *Hey*, the compassionate breath,
says to the surprised and surprising *Dalet*,
"How can I be of service today?"

Chesed is friendly loving-kindness,
like the "*Hey*",
breathing naturally through open spaces
to the heart of the matter,
surprised into service
in awesome ways.

Breathe in the friendliness of the 29th gate
so it becomes a part of you,
and breathe your awesome, awe-filled self
out through the rounded opening.

Gate 30
Gevurah b'Hod / Discipline
within Humility and Splendor

OMER
WEEK 5, DAY 2

OMER TESHUVAH
WEEK 3, DAY 6

What does *gevurah* mean
when powerful human acts
leave us speechless not from trauma
but from the shock of sheer unbridled beauty
at the pathways created in their wake?

Start with your own breath.

Notice each breath as it comes in and out,
gently set aside other thoughts that arise,
let these thoughts know
you will attend to them later.

Become aware of the power of your breath,
how it is given to you as a gift from the air
and given back by you in a constant exchange.

Imagine a most awe-filled place,
then imagine your own breath
carrying you to it
as if you were riding
atop the wings of the Shekhina,
carried along by the Divine Presence herself,
so at the end of the journey you are exhilarated
but not spent,
and are left exalting in the wonder of it all.

Create your own definitions
of power and awe
and ride through the 30th gate

Gate 31
Tiferet b'Hod / Balance
within Humility and Splendor

There's a fountain
with rocks sculpted high
in purposefully odd angles,
forming relationships
that topple and spray water
in all directions.

If you look at one spout
from a certain angle
the spray looks like fireworks
fanning into the sky.

At another spot
in the late afternoon light
a shadow is cast so that the water
seems to manifest from thin air.

You can hike up your pants
and wade in the shallow pool.
If your head gets too hot
you can fill a hat with water, put it on,
and let the cool water soothe you.

The splendor of human ingenuity,
a mere reflection of the natural world,
offers many opportunities
to keep our systems in balance.

How can you use your own ingenuity
to promote balance in your life,
harmony in your spirit,
connection to the world that sustains you?

Invoke a holy intention, a *kavannah*,
as you wade through the 31st gate.

Gate 32
Netzach b'Hod / Endurance
within Humility and Splendor

OMER   **OMER TESHUVAH**
WEEK 5, DAY 4   **WEEK 3, DAY 4**

Rows are hoed neatly in a field
so plants have the proper space to grow
and farmers and farm workers
will have space to harvest.

Words are written in rows
or in columns
so our brains can order them into meaning.

People ordered into rows for too long
can become mechanistic,
stop thinking for themselves.

Still a disciplined team accomplishes more
than an individual
caught running helter skelter.

Hoeing with precision,
crafting clear and beautiful prose,
creating a well-functioning team,
these things take time

and then, *a-ha!*

Tenacity in the service of a fruitful harvest,
the task ahead at the 32nd gate.

Gate 33
Hod b'Hod / Humility and Splendor within Itself

**OMER
WEEK 5, DAY 5**

**OMER TESHUVAH
WEEK 3, DAY 3**

How ya doing
You Splendorous One
who knocks me off my feet?

I hold you in two hands and think
how can this be, with you so vast
and my hands so small?

Today I find myself
wanting to take care of you,
then longing to be enfolded by you.

You wrap around me like Jacob's coat
then turn inside out and decorate my insides
with a broad palette of possibilities.

What could be more amazing than that?

Hod within *Hod*,
the 33rd gate.

Gate 34
Yesod b'Hod / Connection
within Splendor and Humility

OMER
WEEK 5, DAY 6

OMER TESHUVAH
WEEK 3, DAY 2

A woman and her young niece
tie the left shoe of one
to the right shoe of the other.

They link arms and walk awkwardly,
their four feet uncertain how to navigate
this new configuration, their stumbling fueled
by delighted laughter.

They begin to call out, "middle,"
when it is time to move the tied feet,
then "other," for the unbound feet,
and for a brief exhilarating moment
the rhythm carries them along.

The niece says, "Shhh,"
hoping they might keep the rhythm in silence,
which they do for a few short steps,
until their feet get confounded again,
and they stop, sighing and chuckling,
in fun-filled frustration.

Laughter is a kind of *Hod*,
splendorous and humbling,
tying us to our stumbling
and bumbling humanity.

Connection and laughter,
the 34th gate.

Gate 35
Malkhut b'Hod / Divine Presence
within Splendor and Humility

OMER
WEEK 5, DAY 7

OMER TESHUVAH
WEEK 3, DAY 1

The Divine Shekhina
likes to be known.

She paints flowers
and sunsets and moons.
She blows fierce winds
so we'll hear her,
and raises dew gently from the grass
so we'll feel her beneath our feet.

Lately She's been grumbling
that we aren't paying enough attention
and she is not feeling well at all.
Her system is out of balance,
her icy caps are melting too fast,
her waters are falling and spilling
and creating huge torrents,
her temperature is rising.

If only we could take her
to the emergency room,
let the experts bring her fever down
but this illness of the earth
is attacking the very systems
designed to maintain her

We humans are cells
that need to rally on her behalf,
nurture each other, love ourselves well.

What is one thing you can do today
to notice the earth's splendor,
enhance the *malkhut*, the nobility, of another,
or enrich the soil of your own life
with awareness?

Walk through the 35th gate and notice
Shekhina's healing presence.

*Folded paper and light study, Elizheva
Hurvich, 2012.*

Gate 36
Chesed b'Yesod / Loving-Kindness within Connection

**OMER
WEEK 6, DAY 1**

**OMER TESHUVAH
WEEK 2, DAY 7**

Interlacing fingers,
overlapping hands,
arms linked in friendship,
lovers' legs entwined

a colleague's kind acknowledgement,
a stranger's hand reaching
to catch the falling groceries.

With *chesed* we bind ourselves to what's holy
by binding ourselves to each other.

How are you bound
to love today
here at the 36th gate?

Gate 37
Gevurah b'Yesod / Discipline within Connection

**OMER
WEEK 6, DAY 2**

**OMER TESHUVAH
WEEK 2, DAY 6**

"Life takes a lot of courage,"
one holy teacher said.

No one told us there was no handbook,
or explained you have to plumb the depths
before truly appreciating
the exalted heights.

When we were toddlers
and rode piggy-back on grown-up shoulders
laughing delightedly at the sensation
of being at such high altitudes

no one said this feeling wouldn't last forever.

No one said not to worry,
that we could find it again,
if we keep our eyes open,
find the right playmates,
and teachers.

When we become both giddy child
and weight-bearing adult
we can pick ourselves up
on our own shoulders.

Carry yourself with disciplined joy
through this 37th gate,
an opening to playfulness
and wise judgment.

Gate 38
Tiferet b'Yesod / Balance
within Connection

OMER
WEEK 6, DAY 3

OMER TESHUVAH
WEEK 2, DAY 5

Take two opposites,
dark and light,
full and empty,
war and peace.

Set them on the ground and ask,
"where is the middle?"

If you find the middle on the ground
the answer may be murky
or unsatisfying - gray, half full,
a temporary ceasefire.

But if you make these seeming polarities
the base of a triangle that is pointed upward
the answers are much different,
a rainbow of colors,
a delicious sip of possibilities,
a mutual recognition
of shared and unshared needs
held at a height
from which vision can emerge.

What in yourself is at odds?
What in your world
would you like the vision to see clearly?

Climb the hill of potential
from whatever side you are on,
look out from there knowing
you can't reach your vision
without climbing down
in a new direction.

This is the trail
to the 38th gate.

Gate 39
Netzach b'Yesod / Endurance
within Connection

OMER
WEEK 6, DAY 4

OMER TESHUVAH
WEEK 2, DAY 4

How are you connected
to Divine Inspiration?

A tweet, a network,
a digital modem?
A telephone wire?
A string with a tin can
attached to either end?

Is it a tight leather leash
that keeps you online,
or a silk thread barely visible
to the naked eye?

Is it not there at all sometimes.
or just sitting in your pocket
for when you need it?

Is it short, or long,
or indefinable, stretching out endlessly
then retracting as needed?

Most of all
is it sturdy enough to withstand
the tests of a lifetime?

Envision your enduring connection
its size and shape
weight and color
texture and smell.

Carry it with you
as you connect to the other side
of the 39th gate.

Gate 40
Hod b'Yesod / Humility and Splendor
within Connection

OMER   **OMER TESHUVAH**
WEEK 6, DAY 5   **WEEK 2, DAY 3**

No one knows exactly
how the Tailor came up
with the original pattern,
but it cloaks the sky.

Each day we marvel
and thank the Designer
with our very souls
because the cloak She wears
is the world in which we live
and we are tied irrevocably
to Her through this.

She wraps Herself
in splendor and radiant beauty
and when Her arms open
light spreads itself above
and shines among us,
and when She closes Her arms around us
Her darkened depths become our own

and when the fringes of Her garment
tickle the edges of our lives,
we laugh at our choices,
mistakes and misdeeds,
knowing that our saving grace
is in how little we know

and how much we are capable
of learning.

Splendor and humility,
tiny stitches in the garments of gratitude
here at the 40th gate.

Gate 41
Yesod b'Yesod / Connection
within Connection

OMER
WEEK 6, DAY 6

OMER TESHUVAH
WEEK 2, DAY 2

We use the tools at our disposal
to put the pieces back together.

Once the thread broke on a page of Torah
when the scroll was being lifted
to display to the congregation.

Some people were distraught,
some barely noticed,
some were distraught
that others didn't notice.

The lessons from the reading
had been trying that day.

The teacher said,
"let's fix the Torah."

So after lunch
we collected our tools,
a sewing needle,
a magnifying glass,
and a roll of dental floss.

What lightweight items
do you carry when you travel,
and how might they be used
when things you depend on
begin to unravel?

Tuck them away safely
within easy reach, you can always
take them out later, after you cross
through the 41st gate.

Gate 42
Malkhut b'Yesod / Divine Presence within Connection

**OMER
WEEK 6, DAY 7**

**OMER TESHUVAH
WEEK 2, DAY 1**

Most of us can't live
without shoes.

Can we tie our shoes today
or slip them on our feet
with so much holy intention
that we are bound to the Shekhina
through this most basic activity
of daily living?

The sovereignty of *Malkhut*
is represented by the Shekhina,
the earthly manifestation of the Divine
Blessed be Her name.

If we could all walk,
and walked outside barefoot all the time
on smooth ground or soft sand,
we would massage the Shekhina's back
with each step, and she would purr to us
through the spaces between our toes.

Most of us wear shoes
to protect our feet on rugged ground,
support our spines on concrete and hard floors,
accessorize our outfits
to present ourselves well,

keep our feet warm.
Can we also wear our shoes today
as vehicles for Divine Co-creation
carrying us on pathways
toward wisdom and understanding?

May our steps be firm
and the road clear
as we pass through the 42nd gate.

*Folded paper and light study, Elizheva
Hurvich, 2012.*

Gate 43
Chesed b'Malkhut / Loving-kindness within Divine Presence

Consider the elements
required for this journey.

Without *Chesed*,
Gevurah's structure can become harsh.
Without *Gevurah*,
Chesed's kindness can become so soft
it disappears.

Both are needed for the harmony of *Tiferet*
which holds the scaffolding in place
and allows for the enduring quality of *Netzach*.

Without the endurance of *Netzach*
the splendor of *Hod* would be short-lived
and we might not have time to discover
the humility experienced
in the face of *Hod's* awesome power.

Awareness of *Hod* makes it possible
to be bound in *Yesod* with all that is holy
without being bound as slaves,
and our freedom of spirit
carries us towards the majesty
of *Malkhut*.

For today
the realm of creation rests on *Chesed*.
Through acts of random
and not-so-random kindness
we can remember,
kindness is ours, now and forever.

May kindness be a gift
you channel through the Divine
here at the 43rd Gate.

Gate 44
Gevurah b'Malkhut / Discipline
within Divine Presence

OMER **OMER TESHUVAH**
WEEK 7, DAY 2 **WEEK 1, DAY 6**

Gevurah is the fortitude it takes
to march into physical battle
with an enemy who might kill you.
It is also the strength of a horse
determined to pull a heavy plough
across a rutty field.

It is the strength
of a disciplined martial artist
knowing just when, and how,
to approach and retreat,
to move energy, big or small,
into the larger stream,
or round itself until it falls.

And then there is the focused will
to stand against tyranny
without becoming a tyrant,
to advocate for those in need
without mistaking others' needs for our own,
to believe so deeply in justice
that we fight for it justly
without revenge as our motive,
to live our lives each day
knowing how to stand tall in gravity,
to hold one another firmly, lovingly,
from within a deep groove of integrity.

When our disciplined *Gevurah*
is channeled into Life-Affirming Presence
we can tell, we are tilling the soil
for consciousness and new beginnings.

This is our prayer at the 44th gate.

Gate 45
Tiferet b'Malkhut / Balance
within Divine Presence

OMER
WEEK 7, DAY 3

OMER TESHUVAH
WEEK 1, DAY 5

Musical harmony
is a sharing of breath
channeled consciously.

We find harmony with each other
in the mutual awareness that we
and everything around us
are interdependent.

Buddhist *tonglen* practitioners
breathe in pain and suffering
breathe out compassion.
Pain and suffering are transformed
as they travel through the body
through the self.

We can do this in concentric circles,
moving outward, starting with ourselves
and loved ones, then considering
the pain and suffering of others
whom we may not love so much
or know so well,
then all those suffering in the world,
and all the suffering animals,
and the suffering of the planet itself.

Breathe in pain and suffering,
breathe out compassion.

This conscious breath is a prayer
for *Tiferet*, for balance and harmony
within the Divine World,
the Divine Universe.

Inspiration, respiration
and re-inspiration.
This is the 45th gate.

Gate 46
Netzach b'Malkhut / Endurance
within Divine Presence

OMER
WEEK 7, DAY 4

OMER TESHUVAH
WEEK 1, DAY 4

Life, short as it is,
is a long journey.
What gives us endurance
for the duration?

Religious observers of many faiths would say,
"God gives me the strength to go on."
But what happens
when we are not so sure about God?
Or when we don't believe in God at all?
What gives us the strength to re-connect
to the spirit of life and living?

When we practice enduring love
we witness divine presence in our lives.

Netzach is
the endurance of the sun
brilliant, lasting.

Even when night comes
or there is a storm
and the sun goes out of sight,
it is still informing life on earth.

Even if we don't understand
exactly how it works
the sun's rays are required
for us to breathe.

Breathe in the sun's enduring nature
and know it lives in you
even as you breathe it back out.
The plants and trees breathe it in
and recycle it back to you.

This is the 46th gate.

Gate 47
Hod b'Malkhut / Humility and Splendor
within Divine Presence

OMER   OMER TESHUVAH
WEEK 7, DAY 5   WEEK 1, DAY 3

We speak of the still small voice of God,
the one that Jacob heard loud and clear
from within the quiet splendor of his dream,
and when he awoke to the miracle of morning
he looked around and responded,
"God was in this place and I, I did not know..."

A spectacular sunset,
a mountain rising up before us,
waves crashing against the rocks:
sometimes the world overflows with splendor
and we are stunned into silence.

Sometimes the world seems so quiet
we need to listen with extraordinary effort
to notice the beauty that is there.

Sometimes the glitter of life
is easy to mistake for splendor
and we lose sight of humility.

We may live in a world filled with the noise
of cars and buzzing lights, still we can ask,
"Where is the Divine Presence,
here right now?"

This is the irony of *Hod*,
splendor in the simplest things,
and being humbled into the profound silence
at the center of the storm.

Imagine yourself transported there
with all your senses open,
to witness the storm,
hearing there in the stillness
the beginning of a whispered inkling
of what comes next.
This is the 47th gate.

Gate 48
Yesod b'Malkhut / Connection within Divine Presence

OMER
WEEK 7, DAY 6

OMER TESHUVAH
WEEK 1, DAY 2

If you have never put on *tefillin*
to make morning prayers
and even if you have,
consider its intimacy.

We wrap the leather arm strap
attentively seven times,
once for each day of creation, and then
wind it around our middle finger, and say

v'erastich li l'olam,
I will betroth you to me forever
v'erastich li b'tzedek u'v'mishpat,
I will betroth you to me in righteousness
and justice
u'v'chesed, u'v'rachamim,
and loving-kindness and compassion
v'erastich li b'emunah, v'yada-at et Yah,
I will betroth you to me with faithfulness
and in union with these essential qualities
you will know Y-H-V-H,
the Unfolding of Being.

How do we be,
and how do we create,
holy beloveds?

How can we remember
the holiness in difficult times,
the love we know is possible?

Walk through the 48th gate
and notice any answers
that arise throughout the day.

Gate 49
Malkhut b'Malkhut / Divine Presence within Itself

**OMER
WEEK 7, DAY 7**

**OMER TESHUVAH
WEEK 1, DAY 1**

This Gate is *Ha-makom,*
The Place, Divine Presence
in the world around us.

It is Every Place.
It is our shared sovereignty.

Our true human inheritance
is shared nobility
with all people and peoples,
such awe of each other's beauty
that we are humbled and inspired
to abiding love
for the earth that sustains us.

Ha-makom ha-zeh,
this very place you are in,
is noble and you,
can be noble within it.

What are you like as a noble being?
What desires do you have,
what kind of love?
What is your personal task in this life?
What journey are you on?
Who are your fellow and sister travelers?

What can you do today
to demonstrate your own nobility
or unmask the divine spark
in another's eyes?

This is the entry point
to the 49th gate,
to revelation,
and new beginnings.

Folded paper and light study, "Shaft of Wheat," Elizheva Hurvich, 2012.

OMER TESHUVAH

In addition to using the meditations in this book to count the *Omer*, these writings can be used to mark each day between the observance of *Tisha B'Av* and *Rosh ha-Shana*. In this collection, this practice is called *Omer/Teshuvah*, or *Omer Teshuvah*.

Tisha B'Av marks the anniversary of the destruction of the ancient Temple in Jerusalem. The spiritual trek from this time to the New Year represents an opportunity to reconstruct our personal and collective holy sanctuaries through meditation, internal dialog, healing relationships with those we love, and mending our broken world. This period is a time of returning to Divine Love, to more loving relationships others, and to our own best selves. We call this returning *teshuvah*.

One way to do this is to count the 49 days between *Tisha-B'Av* and *Erev Rosh Ha-shana* using the spiritual gateways first presented by Jewish mystics of the sixteenth century. Like with the *Omer*, each day of each week is a time to focus on one of these qualities held within another. We do this in the opposite order of that used for counting the *Omer*, starting with the quality of Divine Presence (*Shekhina)* and moving toward Loving-kindness (*Chesed*).

Enjoy the journey. May it be rich and fulfilling, in whatever directions you may find yourself traveling. Many blessings.

Omer Teshuvah

If you wish to count the days
from *Tisha B'av* to *Rosh HaShana*,
start here.

31657919R00077

Made in the USA
Lexington, KY
21 April 2014